MY MAGIC BREATH

Finding Calm Through Mindful Breathing

WRITTEN BY NICK ORTNER AND ALISON TAYLOR
PICTURES BY MICHELLE POLIZZI

HARPER

An Imprint of HarperCollinsPublishers

My Magic Breath

Text copyright © 2018 by Nick Ortner

Illustrations copyright © 2018 by Michelle Polizzi

For information address HarperCollins Children's Books, a division of HarperCollins Publishers,

195 Broadway, New York, NY 10007.

www.harpercollinschildrens.com

Library of Congress Control Number: 2017939009

ISBN 978-0-06-268776-0

The artist used watercolor on paper to create the illustrations for this book.

Typography by Whitney Manger

18 19 20 21 22   PC/LSCC   10 9 8 7 6 5 4 3 2 1

❖

First Edition

To June and Brenna, who bring magic
into my life every day

—Nick

To Ryan, who has shown me
the magic of a calming breath

—Alison

To River, Rowan, and Nick

—Michelle

Do you have the magic breath?

Let's see . . . Take a deep breath in . . .

The magic breath is special.
It helps when you have too
many thoughts running through
your mind. At the end of a day, there
is a LOT to think about.

Sometimes when you are worried,
or nervous, or sad, deep breaths can
help push some of those thoughts away.
Think about when you feel happy!
Taking a big breath in and thinking about
something that made you feel great
will help you to enjoy your happy moments
even more.

It's magic!

Let's try it out!

What happened today that made you smile?
Take a deep breath in
and picture that moment
in your mind.

Get ready!

Let's blow out all those happy
thoughts onto the page.

Now, that looks like happiness.

Keep blowing! Keep thinking happy!

Whew!
That is a lot of happiness.

I bet you have a smile on your face.
A big smile can make you feel better.

But sometimes things happen that make you feel
sad or mad. Did something happen today
that made you feel that way?
I bet it's stuck in your mind.

Let's try your magic breath again.

Think about what happened.
Now keep it in your mind!

Close your eyes and take a deep breath in.

Now blow out your breath here.

One more time! Take an even bigger breath.
Remember that happy thought?
Use it to push out your sad thought.

Can you blow that sad thought right off the page?

Keep trying!

Make sure to blow all the sad thoughts out of sight!

Whew!

You did it! Good-bye, sad thoughts!
Do you feel better now?

You used your magic breath to help you!

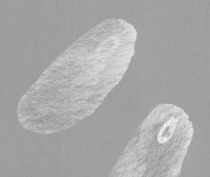

Taking deep breaths in and out when
you are sad, or mad, or worried, or
happy can help you feel better.

Your magic breath can help you laugh and
appreciate happy times! Magic breath can
also help you feel calm when
you are not so happy.

Instead of having your mind full of thoughts
at the end of the day, your mind is ready
for sweet dreams!

Let's do one big yawn together!

Time to give your magic breath a rest.

Sweet dreams . . . Until tomorrow.